⚜⚜⚜

JAMES T. CLELAND has been James
B. Duke professor of preaching and dean
of the chapel at Duke University since
1945. He received the M.A., B.D., and
D.D. degrees from Glasgow University
in Scotland and S.T.M. and Th.D. degrees from Union Theological Seminary
in New York.

Dr. Cleland taught religion at Am-
herst College from 1931 to 1945. He has
also taught summer sessions at Union
Theological Seminary and the Pacific
School of Religion. He is now consultant
to the Chiefs of Chaplains of the three
Armed Forces.

Dr. Cleland contributes sermons regularly to books and periodicals and is a
contributor to *The Interpreter's Bible.*
He is the author of *Wherefore Art Thou
Come?* and *Preaching to Be Understood,*
both published by Abingdon.

HE DIED
AS HE LIVED

❧❧❧

JAMES T. CLELAND

HE DIED
AS HE LIVED

meditations on the seven words

from the cross

ABINGDON PRESS
NEW YORK
NASHVILLE

HE DIED AS HE LIVED

Copyright © 1966 by Abingdon Press

Library of Congress Catalog Card Number: 66-11058

SET UP, PRINTED, AND BOUND BY THE
PARTHENON PRESS, AT NASHVILLE,
TENNESSEE, UNITED STATES OF AMERICA

TO MY COLLEAGUES AND STUDENTS
OF TWENTY YEARS IN THE
DIVINITY SCHOOL OF
DUKE UNIVERSITY

1945-1965

PROLOGUE

There is a story from France which in picturesque fashion represents what we shall try to do in these Good Friday meditations set within the framework of worship. It tells of a boy who, day after day, ran to church during his lunch hour, tiptoed down the central aisle to a front pew, bowed toward the altar, knelt down, and for five minutes gazed at the crucifix. Then he rose, genuflected again, tiptoed out, and took to his heels, back to his work. One day the curé, who had watched this boy's daily devotion for some time, stopped him and asked him, with interest and admiration, just what he was doing. The answer was simple and profound: "I look at Jesus. He looks at me. Then I go back to my work."

That, in plain essence, is what we shall do. We shall look at Jesus. He will look at us. We shall look for twenty minutes, an hour, two hours, three hours. Then we shall go back to our work, remembering him, the man of sorrows who was acquainted with grief, who was wounded for our transgressions, who died to our benefit. Remembering him, we shall wait for Easter, when God put his imprimatur on Jesus of Nazareth, raising him from the dead and giving him the name that is above every name: Jesus Christ the Lord.

But we shall do more than look; we shall listen. We shall listen to the words which Jesus spoke from the cross, seven sentences, to those gathered around the cross: his enemies, a fellow criminal, his mother, the beloved disciple, his God. And we shall discover two things. What he is saying are echoes, repetitions, restatements, applications of what he often said during his teaching ministry. At Calvary he is crossing the t's and dotting the i's of the Sermon on the Mount, and of the parables, and of his chats with individual souls up and down Palestine. More than that, we shall discover that he is talking to us, his friends today, his disciples today, maybe his enemies today. It will not always be easy for us to listen to him. We may be upset. We may want to close our ears. We may even wish that he had not said what he is reported to have said. A Negro spiritual has warned us of what may happen:

8

Were you there when they crucified my Lord?
Were you there when they nailed him to the tree?
Were you there when they laid him in the tomb?
Oh!
Sometimes it causes me to tremble, tremble, tremble.

Yet, perhaps the only way we can enter into the joy of Easter is to have trembled at the cross on Friday, on "Bad" Friday, on Friday which is "Good" only in the light of Easter morning.

So let us go forward to the Seven Words with one prayer constantly in our hearts: that the words of *my* mouth and the meditation of *our* hearts may be acceptable in God's sight, our strength and our redeemer.

So let us pray:

Let the words of my mouth and the meditation of our hearts be acceptable in thy sight, O Lord, our strength and our redeemer. Amen.

THE FIRST WORD

"FATHER, FORGIVE THEM; FOR THEY KNOW NOT WHAT THEY DO."

And as they led him away, they seized one Simon of Cyrene, who was coming in from the country, and laid on him the cross, to carry it behind Jesus. . . .

Two others also, who were criminals, were led away to be put to death with him. And when they came to the place which is called The Skull, there they crucified him, and the criminals, one on the right and one on the left. And Jesus said, "Father, forgive them; for they know not what they do."

—Luke 23:26, 32-34

THE FIRST WORD

Let us look at Jesus; let us listen to him. And let him look at us, with those penetrating, understanding, loving eyes; and let him speak to us as we gather around the cross—some of us very close to it, some of us at a distance, but all within earshot. Let us look honestly. He is not crucified between two candles on an ecclesiastical altar. He is being done to death on a stark, wooden cross between two other criminals outside the holy city at a spot called "the place of a skull." Crucifixion is a cruel form of capital punishment, invented by the Carthaginians and reserved by the Romans as the extreme punishment for criminals of the lowest classes and for slaves and rebels. Probably there was but one more cruel death, also Carthaginian: to be staked out on the desert, face up to the sun, with the eyelids cut off. Crucifixion was never the last penalty for a citizen of Rome. Paul, a citizen, was beheaded.

But tradition has it that Peter was crucified. Like Jesus, he too was an unen-
franchised Jew. Crucifixion was death by
lengthy torture: exposure, exhaustion,
pain, shock. If there is any redeeming
feature to the brutal awfulness of the
transaction, it is that our Lord died in six
hours according to Mark (15:25), or in
three hours according to the Fourth Gospel
(19:14). Beginning about noon, he spoke
seven times before he gave up the ghost at
three o'clock of a Friday afternoon.

✛

According to the church's tradition, which
we shall follow, the first word is: "Father, forgive them; for they know not
what they do." It is hardly what we expect,
even from our Lord, at such a moment.
Think whom he was forgiving. They were
the leaders of the Jews: the high priest,
the Sanhedrin, the Sadducean party which
controlled Jerusalem and led the opposi-
tion to Jesus. They were the Pharisees,
whose passivity allowed the execution, if
their activity did not cause it. They were
the Romans, an army of occupation, who
realized that it was necessary to support
their local allies, if the difficult rule of this
disgruntled church-state was to be possible at all. At a time of emotional religious
tension, such as the Passover, it was po-

14

litically expedient to put one man to death rather than to have a riot, an insurrection, a rebellion, on one's military hands. And Jesus asks God to forgive them all, to wipe out any charge against any of them, to drop any claim to retribution, any desire for legitimate retaliation. He asks God to forget the verse: "Vengeance is mine; I will repay, says the Lord" (Deut. 32:35; Rom. 12:19).

Do you notice the reason he gives for his intercession: They don't know what they're doing. Ignorance, sheer ignorance. They lack knowledge, especially that depth of understanding which is wisdom. It is interesting that the early church emphasized this want of knowledge as the basic cause of Jesus' death. Listen to Peter: "And now, brethren, I know that you acted in ignorance, as did also your rulers" (Acts 3:17). Listen to Paul: "For those who live in Jerusalem and their rulers, because they did not recognize him nor understand the utterances of the prophets which are read every sabbath, fulfilled these by condemning him" (Acts 13:27). Yes, it never dawned on them, Jew or Roman, who this Jesus actually was: Messiah, Son of God. If they *had* known, things would have been different, suggest Peter and Paul. Socrates had said that there is only one evil: ignorance. Goethe is to say that there is

15

nothing more terrible than active ignorance. Yet, even though it killed him, Jesus said of his ignorant opponents: "Father, forgive them."

✠

A few minutes ago I said that such a prayer for forgiveness is hardly what we expect, even from our Lord, at such a moment. Yet maybe I was wrong. When we think of his teaching and his behavior throughout his ministry, forgiveness ought to be what we expect. Listen to three verses from the Sermon on the Mount: "You have heard that it was said, 'You shall love your neighbor and hate your enemy.' But I say to you, Love your enemies and pray for those who persecute you, so that you may be sons of your Father who is in heaven" (Matt. 5:43-45). Forgiveness of an enemy is *the* mark of spiritual sonship. Isn't Jesus running true to form in the first word? I know it is a hard saying for folk like us. Peter once asked Jesus if seven times were sufficient to forgive a brother—not an enemy, but a brother! Jesus suggested that he raise it to seventy times seven, four hundred and ninety (Matt. 18:21-22). I suppose Jesus meant that if Peter did it that often, it would become a habit. But to forgive an enemy, even once! That's rough going, ethically, and tough sledding, spiritually. But Jesus taught it in his lifetime and died in physical agony still expressing it. The church has never forgotten that, like the unknown prophet of the Exile, Jesus "made intercession for the transgressors" (Isa. 53:12).

✠

Does this word say anything to us today? Yes. It speaks to us in grace—that is, in graciousness. For we are Sadducees, and Pharisees, and Roman soldiers; and we, in ignorance, have crucified the Lord—some of us, more than once. Our ignorance is worse than that of his original persecutors. For we are supposed to know who he is. Yet he still makes intercession for the transgressors.

Moreover, when we know who he is and that he forgives, it becomes possible for us to forgive, even when we're being hurt. You are aware that December 25 is Christmas Day. Do you know what day in the Christian year December 26 is? It is the feast of Stephen, the first Christian martyr. His death is remembered within twenty-four hours of the birth of our Lord. Do you know what Stephen's last words were as he was stoned to death: "Lord, lay not this sin to their charge" (Acts 7:60 KJV). Isn't that "Father, forgive them" in other words? A young Pharisee named Saul heard that prayer. Do you know what Augustine said about Saul hearing that prayer? It was the beginning of the conversion of Paul: "If Stephen had not prayed, the church would not have had Paul."

And the prayer goes on down the centuries, because the followers of Christ, strengthened by his spirit, have prayed it. Here is proof in the life of an English soldier who wrote a German mother:

"As a member of a party of Commandos raiding a village in France, it became my duty to kill your son. . . . I earnestly ask your forgiveness, for I am a Christian. . . . I hope I may, some day after the war is over, talk with you face to face."

The German mother received the note several months later, and she wrote the English soldier in turn: "I find it in my heart to forgive you, even you who killed my son; for I too am a Christian. . . . If we are living after the war is over I hope you will come to Germany to visit me, that you may take the place in my home, if only for a time, of my son whom you killed."

Yes, the prayer goes on, and on, and on, world without end. Thanks be to God.

✠

Jesus' death is in accord with his life. He died as he lived. And he lives in the lives

18

of those who pray his first word after him and because of him and through him: "Father, forgive them; for they know not what they do."

Let us pray:

Almighty and Everlasting God,
Slow to anger and of great mercy;
Hear the prayer which thy Son has made on our behalf,
That we may be forgiven our sins and that we, like him, may ask thee to forgive those who have wronged us;
Through the same Jesus Christ, our Lord.
Amen.

THE SECOND WORD

"VERILY I SAY UNTO THEE, TODAY SHALT
THOU BE WITH ME IN PARADISE."

One of the criminals who were hanged railed at
him, saying, "Are you not the Christ? Save
yourself and us!" But the other rebuked him,
saying, "Do you not fear God, since you are under the same sentence of condemnation? And we
indeed justly; for we are receiving the due reward of our deeds; but this man has done
nothing wrong." And he said, "Jesus, remember me when you come in your kingly power."
And he said to him, "Truly, I say to you, today
you will be with me in Paradise."

—*Luke 23:39-43*

THE SECOND WORD

There were three crosses on Calvary, three fellow convicts hanging side by side, three men whose lives did not measure up to the standard set by society for day-in, day-out living. Two of them fell below that standard; they are described as "malefactors," "criminals." One of them rose above the accepted standard. He, too, was a criminal and had to pay the price of his social nonconformity. Unusual goodness may be equally an offense with unusual badness. As we gaze on the cross, it is wise for us to remember that a crime is not necessarily a sin.

✤

We know the charge against Jesus. It was nailed to the cross for all to see and to read: JESUS OF NAZARETH, THE KING OF THE JEWS (John 19:19). For the Romans such an indictment was treason, and the penalty for treason was

death. For the Jews such an accusation
was probably blasphemy, if "King of the
Jews" is equated with "Messiah." The
penalty for blasphemy was death (Lev. 24:
11 ff.). But why were the other criminals
condemned to death? Were they also political prisoners, members of the growing
Zealot movement, who hoped by a revolu-
tionary *coup d'état* to drive Rome out of
Palestine and so inaugurate the kingdom
of God? It would be a dramatic touch if all
three men were hanging on Golgotha because of their belief in the kingdom of God,
because of their Messianic convictions.

One of the two is angry, indignant, con-
sistently self-centered. He picks up the
jeers of the soldiers: "If you are the King
of the Jews, save yourself" (Luke 23:36-
37), and he gives it a new twist: "Are you
not the Christ? Save yourself and us!"
And us! The other rebukes him. He is evi-
dently conscious of a difference between
the cause of their crucifixion and the reason for Jesus' execution. He reproves his
suffering companion: "Steady on. Apart
from the fact that we are guilty and this
man is innocent, aren't you afraid of God?
You ought to be since you are about to die.
Now you make things worse for yourself by
mocking his Messiah." Then he turns to
Jesus and says: "Jesus, remember me
when you come in your kingly power."

This criminal is often referred to as "the penitent thief." But one wonders in what way his plea is primarily a confession of sin? Is it not, rather, an affirmation of confidence? This fellow sufferer on the central cross *is* the Messiah, the inaugurator of the kingdom of God. That kingdom doesn't come in the way the criminal had thought: by political maneuvering and guerilla action. That kingdom is given by God to folk who believe in Jesus' teaching: to the pure in heart; to the poor in spirit; to the peacemakers. The criminal caught on to the idea late and vaguely; but he caught on to something like it. And Jesus promised him more than he asked: "You don't have to wait until the kingdom is established; 'Today shalt thou be with me in Paradise.' " This is mercy in action, the mercy which is the desire and ability to give comfort to the most undeserving.

What is Paradise? What does Jesus mean by Paradise? We do not know. Sheol (or Hades) is the abode of the dead. Gehenna is the suburb of Sheol appointed for the punishment of the wicked. Presumably, Paradise is the suburb of Sheol reserved for the blessed, the accepted of God. Jesus promised that malefactor more than he asked for.

There were three crosses on Calvary. One criminal died *alongside* Jesus; the other died *with* Jesus. There is an eternity of difference in the two prepositions.

✦

"Today shalt thou be with me in Paradise." Isn't it what we would have expected our Lord to say? His answer on the hill of Golgotha is all of a piece with a statement he made on another hill, on the Mount of the Sermon. There he said: "Blessed are the merciful" (Matt. 5:7). Why are they "blessed"? Partly because "they shall obtain mercy." But, more basically, because, by being merciful, they are behaving like God. This deed of mercy on the cross is in line with our Lord's whole ministry. He had praised a father who welcomed his prodigal son home, when the boy didn't deserve it. Mercy. He had said to the woman taken in adultery: "Neither do I condemn you; go, and do not sin again" (John 8: 11). Mercy. When he was asked about who really is one's neighbor, he had told a story which suggests that one's neighbor is anyone in imminent need, as the good Samaritan recognized. Mercy.

A person is merciful when he feels the sorrow and misery of another as if it were his own. Jesus was interested in sinners, not because of their merit but because of their misery. They needed someone like him. That was enough to make him move

into action. Our Lord was not in strange
company on the cross; he had frequented
with sinners all of his life. His enemies
complained that he ate and drank with tax
collectors and sinners (Matt. 11:19). They
even called him a friend of sinners (Luke
7:34), and he wore the nickname like a
badge of honor. He once said: "him who
comes to me I will not cast out" (John
6:37). Why wouldn't he get rid of them?
Because he believed that his Father had
sent them. So his job was to accept them.
You see, he was utterly convinced that
God is merciful, and to be like God is to be
merciful.

*

What does this say to us? Believe it.
Believe it. Believe it. Oh, I know many of
us don't want to believe it. Why should a
criminal, and presumably a sinner, be
granted Paradise at the fifty-ninth minute
of the eleventh hour? There is only one
reason: Jesus said he would, and he said
it because mercy is *the* attribute of God.
William Camden, in his fascinating rem-
iniscences, tells of a man who died in-
stantly when he fell from his horse. There
was speculation as to his ultimate destina-
tion, and "some in this judging World,
judged the worst." A real friend wrote
this epitaph for him:

My friend judge me not
Thou seest I judge not thee:
Betwixt the stirrup and the ground,
Mercy I askt, mercy I found.

That unfortunate rider had even less time
than the pleading criminal. Yet one friend,
who understood the gospel, knew that it
was time enough, that it was possible to
ask and receive mercy "betwixt the stirrup and the ground." Christianity is, as
someone has said, "the religion of all
poor devils." For never forget that we
don't get into heaven because we're good.
We get into heaven because God is good.
Thanks be to God.

✤

Do we ever long for a patron saint, a personal saint, a junior-varsity saint? May I
suggest this criminal, who is known as
Dismas? He is the patron saint of thieves
and robbers and, I read somewhere, of
outfielders in baseball! Bishop Sheen has
suggested that the last thing he stole was
Paradise. May I dare correct a bishop?
Dismas didn't have to steal Paradise; he
received it as a free gift of grace from a
fellow criminal who had the right to make
the gift. The offer is still open.

Let us pray:

Almighty and Eternal God,
Who art full of surprises;
Make us to realize that, since thine is the
    kingdom, thou mayest open it to anyone
    whom thou dost choose,
To the end that even we may be saved;
Through Jesus Christ, our Lord.
Amen.

THE THIRD WORD

"WOMAN, BEHOLD THY SON!
BEHOLD THY MOTHER!"

Standing by the cross of Jesus were his mother, and his mother's sister, Mary the wife of Clopas, and Mary Magdalene. When Jesus saw his mother, and the disciple whom he loved standing near, he said to his mother, "Woman, behold your son!" Then he said to the disciple, "Behold your mother!" And from that hour the disciple took her to his own home.

—John 19:25-27

THE THIRD WORD

Jesus, our Lord, has spoken twice from the cross. He has asked God to pardon his persecutors, his executioners. It is, at one and the same time, a startling and an expected utterance. He had talked about forgiveness during his ministry; but what a moment to echo his teaching! Then he had steadied a fellow criminal by promising him more than he asked or expected: a place beside Jesus in Paradise. This is good news to the very end, as death closed in on Calvary. Now there is a homier, a more intimate touch, to his third word. He speaks to his mother and to a young man. Let us give them our attention.

✤

A group of women had gathered around the cross. They are mentioned by name, without any unanimity, in three of the four Gospels (Matt. 27:55-56; Mark 15:40-41; John 19:25). It is interesting to note that

Mary, the mother of Jesus, is referred to
only in John. Moreover, she is mentioned
in but one other place in the Fourth Gospel,
at the marriage in Cana of Galilee (2:1-5).
She is a figure in the background, almost a
nonexistent figure, for the Fourth Evan-
gelist. He recognizes her once at the beginning of her son's ministry; but he
singles her out for special attention at the
end of Jesus' earthly life. There is a man
with her, but hardly the man we would
have expected. Is he one of her other sons?
No. Is he one of the intimate group of
disciples, known as the Twelve? No. This
latter fact is always a shock to us men.
None of Jesus' closest male companions
stood by him as he was publicly executed.
One, Judas, had betrayed him. Where he
was, no one tells us. One, Peter, had denied
him, in sturdy fisherman's language.
Where he was, no one tells us. The others
had disappeared. The gentler sex, the
weaker sex, shared the death agonies of
the man of Galilee. Yet, to save our mascu-
line face, one man was there, a nameless
man, who is referred to only as "the disciple whom Jesus loved" (John 19:26. cf.
13:23; 20:2; 21:7, 20). Who was he? We
don't know, though tradition has identified
him with John, the son of Zebedee. It seems
more likely, as several New Testament
commentators have suggested, that he was

a young Jerusalemite, maybe with priestly connections, whom Jesus admitted to the intimate fellowship of the Twelve in the last days of the ministry. He first appears, for certain, at the Last Supper: "One of his disciples, whom Jesus loved, was lying close to the breast of Jesus" (John 13:23). He is prominent in the Resurrection and post-Resurrection Johannine narrative. He may have been the author or, at least, the inspirer of the anonymous Fourth Gospel, which we know as "The Gospel According to John." He stood with the women, and Jesus linked him, for eternity, with Mary, the mother of our Lord. He did it with utter simplicity, but with commanding definiteness: He introduced them to each other. He said to his mother: "Woman, behold thy son!" Notice how these four words are punctuated: Woman (*comma*) behold thy son (*exclamation point*). Then he said to the beloved disciple: "Behold thy mother!" and there is an exclamation point there, too. Do you know what the next verse says? "And from that hour that disciple took her to his own home." That is all. But it is sufficient. His mother was looked after. Jesus had kept the fifth commandment, even though its promise was not for him.

Now in a land that invented Mother's Day and surrounds it with all the trimmings of commercial sentimentality, let us notice one devastating fact: Jesus did not give his mother into the care of her family and his; he gave her into the care of the church. That should make us think twice on the second Sunday of May. Maybe it is an idea which is worth further reflection. How shall we go at it?

✤

Let us approach it in this way. It is the thesis of these seven meditations that what our Lord said from the cross is an echo, a reiteration of what he said during his ministry. Can it possibly be true that Jesus subordinated family ties and affection to the demands and the camaraderie of the incipient church? It seems to be so.

There is a passage which occurs in all three Synoptic Gospels where our Lord says some shocking words:

And his mother and his brothers came; and standing outside they sent to him and called him. And a crowd was sitting about him; and they said to him, "Your mother and your brothers are outside, asking for you." And he replied, "Who are my mother and my brothers?" And looking around on those who sat about him, he said, "Here are my mother and my brothers! Whoever does the will of God is my brother, and sister, and mother." (Mark 3:31-35. cf. Matt. 12:46-50; Luke 8:19-21.)

36

And that is that. Jesus' true family were his disciples: his spiritual kith, but not necessarily his blood kin.

This is understandable. John tells us that his brothers "did not believe in him" during his lifetime (7:5). Mark uses stronger language than that. He says that Jesus' familiars thought he was crazy, mad, out of his mind (3:21). Maybe that is why our Lord was forced to dramatize his conception of the new family of God by using as strong a verb as "hate" about one's attitude to one's relatives: "If any one comes to me and does not hate his own father and mother and wife and children and brothers and sisters, yes, and even his own life, he cannot be my disciple" (Luke 14:26). We may try to soften that statement by talking about hyperbole, and poetic license and homiletical exaggeration; but surely we discern his intentional emphasis. The kingdom of God has a priority which may not be usurped by the family. "Mother, I give you into the care of the church. My spiritual son, look after the woman who bore me, for she is standing by me." The family yields to the church, because the church becomes the family.

✤

This third word from the Cross says nothing to some of us, and for a good reason: There is no conflict between our family loyalty and our love for the church. Our parents brought us up "in the nurture and admonition of the Lord." The family table and the family pew are furniture in the *one* home. Good. It is a blessed thing when our earthly kin and our heavenly Father see eye to eye. But to others of us there is a warning in the third word. There is such a thing as a priority in life. God is first, by name, by definition. Does this also mean that the church—the body of Christ, the Son of God—has a claim superior to the family? That would depend on how true the church is to its Lord's life and spirit. But the question should give us pause. The Jesus who made provision for his mother as he died, did so in a fashion embarrassing to some of us but consistent with his experience and teaching.

Let us pray:

Almighty and Eternal God,
Who through thy Son Jesus Christ hast given unto us the church;
Help us to make the church on earth worthy of thy Son,
That it may be a family where all men and women may be thy children and call thee Father;
Through the same Jesus Christ, whose church it is, even thy Son, our Lord.
Amen.

THE FOURTH WORD

"MY GOD, MY GOD, WHY HAST
THOU FORSAKEN ME?"

Now from the sixth hour there was darkness
over all the land until the ninth hour. And about
the ninth hour Jesus cried with a loud voice,
"Eli, Eli, lama sabach-thani?" that is, "My
God, my God, why hast thou forsaken me?"
—*Matt. 27:45-46*

THE FOURTH WORD

Does the care of his mother in the third word lead naturally and inevitably to Jesus' cry to his Father in the fourth word? Did those who first assigned a consecutive order to the seven sayings have any purposeful reason for juxtaposing "Woman, behold thy son!" and "My God, my God, why hast thou forsaken me?" The exclamation point is followed by a question mark; the assertion is followed by a doubt.

This is the word which one reluctantly examines. For one thing, there is an alarming aspect to it: According to Matthew and Mark, it is the *only* saying from the cross. For these two evangelists Jesus' last words were: "My God, my God, why hast thou forsaken me?" The overt terror is enough to frighten the commentator. For another thing, the consternation leads to bewilderment, as James Stalker pointed out years ago: "In the entire Bible there is no other sentence so difficult to explain. The first

thought of a preacher, on coming to it, is
to find some excuse for passing it by, and,
after doing his utmost to expound it, he
must still confess that it is quite beyond
him.'' Yet we must examine this excruciating word. It is literally ''excruciating''—
ex cruce: ''from the cross''—which being
interpreted is ''exquisitely, acutely, and
unbearably painful.''

✠

That this word is genuine there is little
question. It is the one saying remembered
in Jesus' native tongue, Aramaic: *''Eli,
Eli, lama sabach-thani?''* ''My God, my
God, why have you abandoned me, deserted
me, left me helpless?'' It is not the kind of
dying comment which the church would
have invented for its Lord. It was a shock
for the hearers—that this God-conscious
man should be bereft of his divine main-
stay. It was a shock for the evangelists—
two of them dropped it altogether. It is
still a shock for interpreters. What did
Jesus mean? Let us look together at some
possible answers.

The simplest interpretation is that it did
not mean anything. It was a cry of delirium
and, therefore, cannot be expected to make
sense. Or, it was a cry of agony. The cross
hurt. Jesus' racked body gave vent to this
tortured, tormented ejaculation, and

nothing should be read out of it or into it. Yet, it would be an act of expository cowardice to leave it at that.

A second interpretation has a long theological heritage. The fourth word is a cry of abandonment. God hid his face from Jesus, deliberately and of necessity. On the cross Jesus was the scapegoat bearing the sin and the guilt of all mankind. Since God is of too pure eyes to behold iniquity (Hab. 1:13), he had to avert his gaze from his stricken Son who in utter solitude and awful agony made the once-for-all atonement for the sins of the whole world. Paul put the matter very simply and definitely: Jesus was made sin for us, he who knew no sin (II Cor. 5:21). This explanation has some great names behind it: Augustine and Calvin, to mention but two. It has an honored history and a wide acceptance. But, despite my deference to tradition, I cannot accept it. Such a God is not the Father of the prodigal son story. It was not this kind of Supreme Being of whom Jesus taught.

A third interpretation swings to the opposite extreme by looking upon this saying as a cry of faith. It points out that this is the first verse of Psalm 22, which is a hymn of faith, ending up with enthusiasm for the God who vindicates the despairing sufferer

and reestablishes him in companionship.
Vs. 24 reads:

> For he [God] has not despised or abhorred
>   the affliction of the afflicted;
> and he has not hid his face from him,
>   but has heard, when he cried to him.

This psalm has a good history of constant
use by the righteous among the Jews in the
midst of adversity. Yet, I have my doubts
about this optimistic explanation. Does a
dying man quote? Even if the answer is
"yes," does he quote vs. 1, when what he
wants is vs. 24? This exposition is a heroic
and praiseworthy misunderstanding. It is
hardly an unbiased appraisal.

What are we left with? Let me offer a
tentative explanation, remembering James
Stalker's words, already quoted, that how-
ever one expounds the fourth word "he
must still confess that it is quite beyond
him." A fourth interpretation is that this
is a cry of failure and, therefore, of desolation. It is the spoken ache of one who
thought of himself as a deserted man of
God. This is the blackout of faith, the dark
night of the soul. Jesus had failed in
Galilee; he had to flee the country. He had
failed in Jerusalem; the authorities had
neither accepted his teaching nor recognized his messiahship. He had then al-

44

lowed himself to be arrested, tried, and crucified, without any defense, believing the issue was in God's hands. Supposing he is wrong again; then he has really, finally failed. For death is placing its arm around him. The curtain is falling on his ministry and on himself. It has been a destructive conflict, a most unsatisfactory drama—a tragedy. We can almost hear him whisper: "If I looked after my mother, why doesn't my Father look after me?" This word is a cry of abandonment, the import and pathos of which we cannot really grasp because none of us has ever known a similar friendship with God.

✤

Now you have a good question immediately to ask me: "In the first three words you have validated the cries from the cross by reference to the teaching ministry of Jesus. Your refrain has been: 'He died as he lived.' Can you support this interpretation of the fourth word as a cry of failure from anything Jesus said before?" No, I reluctantly admit, not in parallel, definitive quotation. But there are numerous hints at puzzlement, anxiety, questioning, failure. The Fourth Gospel tells us that, on one occasion, many of his followers deserted him because his teaching made no sense to them. He asked the Twelve, almost

45

pathetically: "Will you also go away?"
Peter steadied him in that situation (6:66-
70). In the same Gospel he talked about his
soul being "troubled," and prayed:
"Father, save me from this hour." God
steadied him then (12:27-28). In Luke he
refers to his mission as a "baptism," which
suggests being drowned in death. If he ever
thought of John the Baptist and his end,
Jesus must have had some inkling that a
similar fate awaited him (12:49-53). And
in the Garden of Gethsemane we are told
that he "began to be greatly distressed"
("sore amazed" is the King James trans-
lation), and actually asked God to take
away "this cup" (Mark 14:32-36). Was it
the cup of death? He rallied sufficiently to
add: "Yet not what I will, but what thou
wilt."

The ministry of Jesus was no saunter
down a country lane amid the lilies of the
field, but rather a fight to the death with
real forces of evil. It was a risky, desperate
business, in which he saw himself winning
countless skirmishes, yet never certain that
he was victor in the war. When we realize
that, then it is not blasphemous, and it
may not be presumptuous, for us to consider "My God, my God, why hast thou
forsaken me?" as a cry of failure and of
desolation.

✤

What does this word say to us today? It says that at least once a year it is good for us post-Resurrection Christians to stand on the *other* side, the "Bad" Friday side, of Easter. We subsequently know that God had not forsaken Jesus; the Resurrection was the mighty proof of this. That is why we worship today. God vindicated Jesus. But what did "My God, my God, why hast thou forsaken me?" mean to Jesus and to those who heard him when he spoke the words on a Friday afternoon outside a city wall? They tell us that the Incarnation, the enfleshment, was actual, genuine, authentic, down-to-earth. Our Lord was a mere man; "and being found in human form he humbled himself and became obedient unto death, even death on a cross" (Phil. 2:8)—betrayed, deserted, doubting, desolate.

Let us pray:

Almighty and Eternal God,
Whose blessed Son didst become man;
Assist us to believe that our human lot was his,
That we may know him as our brother as well as our Lord;
Through the same Jesus Christ, thy Word become flesh.
Amen.

❧❧❧❧

THE FIFTH WORD
"I THIRST."

After this Jesus, knowing that all was now
finished, said (to fulfil the scripture), "I thirst."
A bowl full of vinegar stood there; so they put
a sponge full of the vinegar on hyssop and held
it to his mouth.

—John 19:28-29

THE FIFTH WORD

For several years now at the Three Hours service in the Duke University Chapel on Good Friday, the seven meditations, for the most part, have been delivered by laymen: an athletic coach; a professor of botany; teachers in the law school, in the school of engineering, and in the other faculties. Some are men, some are women. Perhaps it is the fact that they are willing to speak at such a time from the chapel pulpit, as much as what they say, which impresses the university community, though memorable things are said. One year a member of the medical school spoke on the fifth word. He is a noted neurosurgeon, who for a time was dean of the medical school and is now vice-provost of the university in the area of medical affairs. In the course of his address he commented that the two sayings from the Cross which a doctor or a nurse hears most often in a hospital ward are: "My God, my God, why hast thou forsaken me?" and "I thirst.'' These are the vocal symptoms of spiritual and physical distress. Our Lord spoke both of them.

It is extremely difficult, if not well-nigh impossible, for those of us who are Protestant to appreciate the Roman Catholic statuary which depicts Jesus the Christ, bearing on his hands and feet the prints of the wounds, in his side the mark of the spear, and in his heart the bloodiness of its breaking. We are apt to dismiss it all as gaudy, tawdry, and cheap. We prefer an empty cross to a crucifix. Maybe we are basically right in such a reaction, except on one day in the year: Good Friday. On that day it is well for us to concentrate on the pain, the anguish of our Lord; otherwise, we may miss something very vital in the faith and for our faith. Jesus suffered; he suffered terribly; he died in physical agony. These were spikes, not brads, which pierced his flesh; they were driven home with a sledgehammer, not with a tackhammer. Into the open wounds settled the insect life of dusty, dirty Palestine. The rostrum from which our Lord spoke his last words was a gallows; his pulpit was a harsh, rugged, wooden cross.

✤

He said: ''I thirst.'' Do you wonder? It had been eighteen hours or more since his last meal, his last supper. He had endured the agony of Gethsemane, the betrayal, the arrest, the cross-examination, the trial, the scourging, the weary walk to Calvary, the crucifixion, the exposure in the sun. And his parched body cried out: "I'm thirsty." Someone acted like a nurse or a doctor and pressed a wet sponge against his lips.

The Gospels are confused and contradictory about this deed of mercy, and some commentators think he may have been given something to drink *twice*. It was a Jewish custom to offer a crucified criminal wine mixed with an opiate to make him unconscious. Perhaps the pious women of Jerusalem prepared such a potion to offset the aching torture of such a death. Jesus seems to have refused it when it was given him. He preferred the Father's Gethsemane cup to this drink. But, according to the Fourth Gospel, when he cried "I thirst," someone soaked a sponge in vinegar, put it on the end of a stick, and held it to his mouth. The Roman troops had a drink made of water, sour wine, and egg: *posca*. Was it a soldier, in a foreign army of occupation, who acted thus? Jesus sipped it. Perhaps an old warrior or a young recruit is in heaven today because he gave "a cup of cold water" in love, expecting no reward.

Why would so human, so elementary, so

everyday a pair of words as ''I thirst'' be remembered among the sayings from the cross? There is a serious, tremendous, never-to-be-forgotten reason. It is to drive home the fact that the Jesus who died at Calvary was a man, a real man, a thirsty human being, whatever else he was. A heresy soon arose in the early church that Jesus was not a man, that his human nature was an illusion, that the Jesus of the ministry did not really die on the cross. It is known as the Docetic heresy. John will have nothing to do with this point of view. He is well aware that Jesus is the unique Word (the *Logos*) of God, who was in the beginning with God. He says so in the opening words of his Gospel (1:1-3). But he adds ''And the Word became flesh and dwelt among us'' (vs. 14). Now he tells us that fleshly Word said: ''I thirst.'' Why not? His was bone like our bone, and flesh like our flesh. Jesus was not God in a human mask. He was God incarnate, enfleshed, thirsty.

✤

Can we support this earthly aspect of our Lord from the years of the teaching ministry? Of course we can. He said to the woman at the well of Samaria, ''Give me a drink'' (John 4:7). He teased Martha about being too fussy over the preparation of a meal, suggesting that only one course was necessary (Luke 10:38-42). But one course was necessary. He was accused of being a glutton and a winebibber (Matt. 11:19), and he never seems to have denied it. He probably wasn't; yet he was no ascetic. He made a wedding party into a success, when it threatened to be a failure, a domestic calamity, by turning water into wine (John 2:1-11). He fed the five thousand, as well as preaching to them (John 6:1-13). He took care of sick bodies. One of the post-Resurrection stories even tells of his preparing a fire and fish and bread for a seaside breakfast for his disciples (John 21: 9). His teaching is full of bread and fish and cold water. The memorial meal his followers continued is focused on bread and wine, the staples of food in Palestine. He rested when he grew weary; he slept through a storm on the Sea of Galilee; he took "time-out" regularly. It need not surprise us that on the cross he said, "I thirst." He died as he lived.

✙

What does this mean for us? It suggests, it emphasizes, it insists that we really believe in the doctrine of the Incarnation. Our Lord is "very God of very God." Yes, but he was, in the days of his flesh, very man of very man. Athanasius applies to him the words "perfect God and perfect man," and "perfect" must be understood with consistency in both usages. If Jesus had to share the divine nature in order to reveal *God* to man, he had also to share our human nature to be the revealer of God to *man.* He was *born,* not uniquely constructed. He really suffered; he did not pretend, make believe, pose. He *died*—dead as a doornail. It is both heretical and absurd to separate the spiritual from the material on this planet. If we do detach them, then the spiritual becomes rarefied, and the material becomes secular. The church holds the two in conjunction; and the adjective for the spiritual and the material in conjunction is "sacramental." So the Incarnation has something to tell us about diapers; the ministry of Jesus has something to tell us about work and hunger and sickness and outcasts; and the Crucifixion has something to tell us about the demands of the body. And when we put them all together, we realize that in the church militant we dare not, we cannot, separate the soul and the body.

♣

The fourth word and the fifth word are confirming footnotes to the doctrine of the Incarnation. Jesus was one of us. The fourth word is his cry of spiritual anguish; the fifth word is his cry of physical pain. He was not "Man" with a capital "M." He was a first-century Palestinian Jew. This is the key to an understanding of both "My God, my God, why hast thou forsaken me?" and "I thirst."

Let us pray:

Almighty and Eternal God,
Who hast conjoined the spiritual and the material in one sacramental union;
Teach us that our bodies are the temples of thy Spirit,
That we may respect and honor our bodies;
As did thy Son, even Jesus Christ, our Lord.
Amen.

THE SIXTH WORD

"IT IS FINISHED."

When Jesus had received the vinegar, he said,
"It is finished"; and he bowed his head and
gave up his spirit.

—John 19:30

THE SIXTH WORD

One of the advantages of being a professor
is that, now and again, an interesting book
lands on one's desk, for review purposes,
which one would never think of buying.
Such a volume is a *Dictionary of Last
Words,* compiled by Edward LeComte.
There are hundreds of final sayings here,
alphabetically arranged, from Robert Ab-
bot, a bishop of Salisbury, to Ulrich
Zwingli, the Swiss reformer, who died at
the battle of Kappel. Interested in what
was chosen as the last word of our Lord,
I turned to the citation under "Jesus
Christ" and found that the editor had,
conservatively and cannily, listed three
sayings: "My God, my God, why hast thou
forsaken me?" the only cry from the cross
in Matthew and Mark; "Father, into thy
hands I commend my spirit," the last of
the three words in Luke; and "It is
finished," the last of the three sayings in
John. We shall continue to follow the ac-

cepted, traditional order and consider "It is finished," to be the sixth rather than the seventh word.

✣

With his thirst relieved by a friendly hand pressing a moist sponge against his lips, Jesus speaks again: "It is finished." That might have been said by other folk than Jesus. The Romans and the Jewish hierarchy could have said it with relief, even joy. The Greek rendition is in a single word, Τετέλεσται the perfect tense of the passive voice of the verb: "it is over and done with," "Curtains!" The followers of Jesus —Mary his mother, the other women, the beloved disciple, who watched him and who watched with him—could have said it. So could the disciples who fled. *"Finis."* But it was Jesus who said it, and one wishes to know the tone of voice in which it was said: relief? disappointment? resignation? exaltation? To know that would be a clue to an understanding of the words.

For what was finished? We are not told. Was it his life on earth? That was almost gone; his body was about to decline to accept any more. He was dying young, though he may have seemed to be older than thirty-three. Some Jews puzzled by his teaching, which had an amazing disregard of time as ordinary man thinks of time, had once said to him: "You are not yet fifty years old, and have you seen Abraham?" (John 8:57). He may have looked older than he was. Yet, even in dying, he would not say, like Hamlet: "The rest is silence" (V, ii). Jesus agreed with the Pharisees on one item of faith: There is continuing life after death.

"It is finished." What is finished? Was it the contents of the Gethsemane cup? He hadn't wanted to drink it; but he was willing to drain it if that was what God wanted: "Not my will, but thine, be done" (Luke 22:42). According to Luke, Jesus had sweated blood to say that (vs. 44); but he had said it. What was in the cup? Duty? Death? Whatever it was, it was God's concoction. That was enough for Jesus. He drank it, to the dregs.

"It is finished." What was finished? Was it the job he came to do? Was this word his own answer to the doubts expressed in the fourth word? If it were that, then he died in blessedness, if not in happiness. Think of dying with one's job done. Death is then of almost no consequence. John Buchan, Lord Tweedsmuir, ends one of his adventure novels with a single sentence about the hero: "There only remained the trivial business of dying."

Yes, death is no great matter—though dying may be a nuisance or a misery—if one can say: "Mission accomplished."

But we are still in the dark, in ignorance as to what the "it" is in "It is finished." Let us turn to his ministry to find if our Lord casts any light on this enigmatic saying.

✦

According to the one story we have of Jesus' youth, he felt, even before he was a teenager, that God had a job for him to do. To his parents who had mislaid him in Jerusalem and failed to find him for three days he said either "Did you not know that I must be in my Father's house" (Luke 2:49), or "Wist ye not that I must be about my Father's business" (KJV). That emphasis is repeated with regularity and urgency, especially in the Fourth Gospel: "My food is to do the will of him who sent me, and to accomplish his work" (4:34), "My Father is working still, and I am working" (5:17), "We must work the works of him who sent me, while it is day; night comes, when no one can work" (9:4). And on the night in which he was betrayed, in the high priestly prayer, in intercession for the Twelve, and in self-dedication, Jesus said: "I glorified thee on earth, having accomplished the work which thou

gavest me to do'' (17:4). Does that petition
anticipate, portend ''It is finished,'' by less
than twenty-four hours?

Jesus was a man under authority. He
had been given a job; he kept at it; he com-
pleted it. He was God's servant, God's suffering servant. But he was a *willing* servant, because he accepted the responsibility
as the rightful demand of a father upon a
son, of his Father upon the Son. Do you
remember the reply of the French soldier
to the surgeon who was commiserating
with him because he had lost a leg in the
war? He answered: ''I didn't *lose* my leg;
I *gave* my leg.'' Jesus said something like
that: ''The Father loves me, because I lay
down my life. . . . No one takes it from me,
but I lay it down of my own accord'' (John
10:17-18). When he said, ''It is finished,''
he was dying as he lived.

But what was the job? To preach the
gospel; to reveal God in action on man's
behalf; to speak the truth in love; to inaugurate the kingdom of heaven; to recon-
cile man to God, to God who was ready,
anxious, working for reconciliation. He
died at the age of thirty-three doing that,
looking as if he were fifty. What God had
asked of him had been accomplished, so far
as Jesus could accomplish it.

✛

Do you grasp what that says to us, if we are his followers? Carry on the mission. How? By simple, humble, everyday acts of lovingkindness. One of the most stupendous juxtapositions in the Fourth Gospel is the combining of two seemingly incompatible, discordant sayings. The first is this: "Jesus, knowing . . . that he had come from God and was going to God. . . ." What would you expect to follow that? "He prayed"; "He committed himself to the Father"; "He gave up the ghost." Do you know what does come next? "[He] laid aside his garments, and girded himself with a towel. Then he poured water into a basin, and began to wash the disciples' feet" (13:3-5). Jesus, knowing he was in a unique relation with God, did a menial, dirty job in love. That is the gospel in deed. John the Elder, almost at the end of his life, was carried into his church at Ephesus for a final word to his congregation. All he said was: "Little children, love one another."

And as we love one another and our enemies, let us remember that we may be hurt, wounded, killed, in the Congo, at Selma, anywhere, anytime. Maybe Paul was hinting at that when he said: "Now I rejoice in my sufferings for your sake, and in my flesh I complete what is lacking in Christ's afflictions for the sake of his body, that is, the church" (Col. 1:24). Maybe Paul wrote his own epitaph: "I have fought the good fight, I have finished the race, I have kept the faith" (II Tim. 4:7). Maybe we—some of us—will be able to say to God as we die: "Mission accomplished."

✠

"It is finished." Yet, it wasn't finished. It was finished so far as Jesus was concerned. But God still had a job to do, for Jesus and on Jesus. That is why Easter follows Friday—and makes it "Good" Friday.

Let us pray:

Almighty and Eternal God,
Who hast given us wills to serve thee as well as minds to know thee and hearts to love thee;
Discipline our wills to obey thy will,
That we may follow in the footsteps of thy Son to whatever end is ours;
Through the indwelling of his spirit,
even Jesus Christ, our Lord.
Amen.

THE SEVENTH WORD

"FATHER, INTO THY HANDS
I COMMEND MY SPIRIT."

It was now about the sixth hour, and there was
darkness over the whole land until the ninth
hour, while the sun's light failed; and the curtain of the temple was torn in two. Then Jesus,
crying with a loud voice, said, "Father, into thy
hands I commit my spirit!" And having said
this he breathed his last.

—Luke 23:44-46

THE SEVENTH WORD

For most of us "It is finished" would seem
to be a final word, the last word. Whatever
Jesus' earthly job was, it was done. Anything else said would run the risk of being
an anticlimax—unimportant, undignified,
even ridiculous. But our Lord has one more
thing to say, one more thing to do. He says
it; in saying it, he does it. He is speaking
for the last time in the days of his flesh.
What will he say? Listen: "Father, into
thy hands I commend my spirit."

✣

Has Jesus in the seventh word returned
to his mother's knee in memory? Is he remembering a psalm which Mary taught
him as a boyhood prayer, Psalm 31? Here
are the first five verses:

In thee, O Lord, do I seek refuge;
  let me never be put to shame;
  in thy righteousness deliver me!
Incline thy ear to me,
  rescue me speedily!

Be thou a rock of refuge for me,
    a strong fortress to save me!
Yea, thou art my rock and my fortress;
    for thy name's sake lead me and guide me,
take me out of the net which is hidden for me,
    for thou art my refuge.
Into thy hand I commit my spirit;
    thou hast redeemed me, O Lord, faithful God.

This is a prayer of trust and of confidence. Maybe it reminds us of a prayer which we learned as children, which we still sometimes pray as adults, when we are tired and weary and have not the words or the time or the energy to say anything else:

This night I lay me down to sleep,
I pray thee, Lord, my soul to keep.
If I should die before I wake,
I pray thee, Lord, my soul to take.

Yet there was a difference in Jesus' situation and in the psalmist's. The psalmist was asking for deliverance *from* physical death; Jesus was asking for acceptance *in* physical death. Jesus was looking beyond this earthly life; it was almost over. He was entrusting his spirit to the care of God, *in extremis*. Moreover, he added one word, one important word, one personal word to the fifth verse of the psalm: *"Father,* into thy hands I commit my

72

spirit." The voluntarily exiled son was going back home.

This seventh word has been referred to as "a proclamation of victory." I hardly think so. Victory is postponed until Easter. It is rather a proclamation of assurance. Jesus has rallied from the despair of "My God, my God, why hast thou forsaken me?" and from the distress of "I thirst." The final word is spoken from strength rather than from weakness, from confidence rather than bewilderment, from peace rather than turmoil. He has done all he could on earth for God: "It is finished." Now he gives himself over to the care of God, to the Father with whom he had always been in contact. It is good to know that our Lord died in confident trust.

✦

It is not surprising—in fact, it is completely in character—that this God-conscious man should have been very conscious of God as his life ebbed from him. We have noticed that, at the age of twelve, he was aware that he was God's Son in an unusual way. When his parents found him after a three-day search in Jerusalem, his mother said to him: "Son, why have you treated us so? Behold, your father and I have been looking for you anxiously." Jesus picked up one word from his mother's wor-

ried question and gave it a new twist:
"How is it that you sought me? Did you
not know that I must be in my Father's
[*my Father's*] house?" (Luke 2:48-49).
God the Father is the pivot around which
the Sermon on the Mount swings: "If you
then, who are evil, know how to give good
gifts to your children, how much more will
your Father who is in heaven give good
things to those who ask him?" (Matt.
7:11). More than once in the Fourth Gospel, he states very simply and assuredly:
"The Father loves the Son" (3:35; 5:20.
cf. 10:17, 29). At the Last Supper he told
the Twelve: "I shall not drink again of this
fruit of the vine until that day when I drink
it new with you in my Father's kingdom"
(Matt. 26:29). In the high priestly prayer,
on the night of the betrayal, he told God
the Father: "Now I am coming to thee"
(John 17:13).

That which lay nearest Jesus' heart, that
which was etched in the deep places of his
spirit, was what gained utterance in the
seventh word. He knew whereof he spoke,
he knew him to whom he spoke, when he
said with a dying shout: "Father, into thy
hands I commit my spirit."

✢

What will *our* last words be? If we are
compos mentis, won't they be in line with

the tenor of our lives? That has been true
of many others. When Mary I of England,
"Bloody Mary," lay dying in 1558, all she
could think of was that Calais, the last
English possession in France, had been
lost during her reign. Her last recorded
words were: "When I am dead and opened,
you shall find Calais lying upon my heart."
In 1931 the dying Anna Pavlova recalled
her greatest triumph as a ballerina and
cried, as her last words: "Get my swan
costume ready."

Where a person's treasure is, there will
his heart be also. Where is our treasure?
Where is our heart? What would our last
words tell? The amazing thing about Jesus'
last word was that it was not said on Calvary once and for all, never to be repeated.
It was taken up and reiterated with confidence by his followers, so that it echoes
again and again down the centuries right
into this year of grace. "Into thy hands I
commend my spirit" were the last words
of Peter, martyr and saint, and of
Charlemagne, the emperor, and probably
of John Huss at the stake, and of Melanch-
thon, the reformer. They were the dying
affirmation of Christopher Columbus in a
wretched hired lodging in Spain and of
Lady Jane Grey on a scaffold in the Tower
of London. Mary, Queen of Scots, and John
Knox, bitter political and religious ene-

mies, both turned to God in their final hours with the last words of the Lord, whom they served so faithfully but so differently.

Time would fail me to tell of the others, heroes and vagabonds of the faith, men and women of the church, unknown to us or well-known to us, of every generation and ours, who died in confidence—confidence, not of trumpets sounding on the other side, but of One who would receive their spirits as he had received his own Son.

✣

"Father, into thy hands I commend my spirit." It is the right note on which our Lord crossed the Jordan. It is the right note on which to close a Good Friday vigil, because it leaves the whole matter with God.

Let us pray:

Almighty and Eternal God,
Creator of our lives and guide of these our pilgrim days;
Grant each one of us the confidence and faith of thy Son,
That our last thoughts and words may be: "Father, into thy hands I commend my spirit";
Through the same Jesus Christ, our Lord. Amen.

76

EPILOGUE

Have you ever seen a criminal die? In
1960, while on a mission with the army in
Europe, I visited the battlefield of Verdun,
that bloody scene of endless carnage in
World War I. An American major was my
guide. In the course of a quite desultory
conversation I asked the officer what he
considered his most interesting experience
in the armed forces. His answer was im-
mediate and unforgettable: "I saw Göring
die." As a young second lieutenant he had
been the officer in charge of escorting the
condemned prisoners from their cells to
the gallows after World War II. Just before zero hour, Göring had outwitted his
legal executioners by committing suicide.

World War I, World War II, Korea,
Viet Nam. Yes, we live in a soldiers' world,
for better or for worse. But so did Jesus.
There are three officers of the Roman army
who are enshrined in the pages of the New
Testament. The first one, stationed at Ca-

pernaum, was given the highest compliment which Jesus ever paid anyone: "Truly, I say to you, not even in Israel have I found such faith" (Matt. 8:10). The second—by name, Cornelius—stationed at Caesarea, was the first non-Jew to become a Christian. Peter brought him into the church, to the embarrassment of the conservatives in Jerusalem. The third officer saw Jesus die. He was the centurion, the second lieutenant, in charge of the Crucifixion. Let us read about him, as the story is recorded by Mark: "And Jesus uttered a loud cry, and breathed his last. . . . And when the centurion, who stood facing him, saw that he thus breathed his last, he said, 'Truly this man was a son of God' " (15:37, 39). Imagine this officer as an old man, reminiscing about his years of service, recalling the Crucifixion and saying: "You know, I saw Jesus die. The only way I can account for him is to say that he was no ordinary man. He was a son of God." Perhaps that officer, once in service in a foreign land, never forgot the crucifixion of a good man.

✦

Like the centurion, we have been watching Jesus die. We have looked at him; he has looked at us. He has spoken; we have heard; we have tried to understand what

he said. For us, too, he is no ordinary man.
He is a prophet, or the Messiah, or the
Lord, or a son of God, or the Son of God,
or the Second Person of the blessed Trin-
ity. And we are remembering that on Good
Friday he died. It is a sad fact, a tragic
fact, an offensive fact. But be of good
cheer. We shall celebrate Easter; and we
may celebrate it the better because, with
the centurion, we have watched Jesus die.

Let us pray:

Almighty and Eternal God,
Whose blessed Son walked in and through the
valley of the shadow of death;
Bless what has been said for the good of thy
worshiping people,
To the end that our Good Friday sorrow may
be transformed into the joy of Easter;
Through the risen and indwelling spirit of the
same Jesus Christ, our Lord.
Amen.